That's My New Friend

Written by Lola Adebayo

Illustrated by Winda Mulyasari

Book design by Lola Adebayo
Illustrations by Winda Mulyasari

ISBN 978-1-8380954-1-3 (paperback)
ISBN 978-1-8380954-0-6 (hardback)

First published in August 2020

Published by Amel & Amira Publishing
www.twinventures.co.uk

Amel & Amira
.PUBLISHING.

In loving memory of my Goddaughter Kayla.

Today was our first day at big school. Our hair was styled really pretty, and our backpacks were so cool.

My backpack was bright pink with flowers,
and mine was purple with a matching lunchbox.

We both had beautiful black shiny shoes
with white frilly socks.

"Are you excited to start school?"
Mummy turned to us to say.

"Oh yes!" we said.
"But what will we get up to today?"

"Well, you'll have lots of fun reading, writing and making new friends." Mum said.
"And don't forget your new notebooks, you left them on your bed."

We held each other's hand and headed out
the door, laughing and skipping all the way.

How excited are we to start big school,
oh it's going to be such a good day!

When we got to the gate mum dusted our dresses and straightened my glasses. She walked us to our classrooms and said "Ok girls, remember you're in different classes."

Our faces grew worried, and our stomachs started doing flips like acrobats at the circus.

"Don't worry, you will see each other at playtime so no need to feel nervous."

The classroom walls were filled with numbers, letters and colourful drawings.

There were activity tables with many things to do, it looks like big school isn't boring.

The teacher said "Amel would you like to play with the building blocks over there?"

I ran over to the blocks where I sat next to a girl
with a huge smile and a big bow in her hair.

"My name is Kayla" she said as she stacked her blocks
so high. "I'm Amel" I said quietly, I was feeling rather shy.

In the other classroom,
"Playtime!" the teacher shouted so all
the children ran outside.

But I was too busy drawing a picture for Amel,
it was going to be a big surprise.

I went outside into the playground and looked around to try and find Amel.

There she is! By the hula hoops under the tree, but who is that other girl?

They were having so much fun
giggling and playing under the tree.

It made me feel sad,
because Amel had forgotten
all about me.

I folded up my surprise and with a sad face started to walk towards the teacher. "What's wrong Amira?"
I pointed at the girl and said "She took my twin sister"

By the tree, we looked over and saw Amira standing with the teacher.

So I grabbed Kayla's hand and we ran over there to see her.

We gave each other a massive hug and I said
"I missed you" And this is my new friend Kayla,
she wants to be your friend too.

Kayla took our hands and dragged us both
to the hula hoops under the tree.

And just like that our friendship of two turned into
a friendship of three!

CPSIA information can be obtained
at www.ICGtesting.com
Printed in the USA
LVHW072326180321
681907LV00011B/218

9 781838 095406